The self-care guide to being your own best friend

# ME TIME

Jessica Sanders
Art by Stephanie Spartels

FIVE MILE

For Mum, Dad, Beck and Bell – JS

Made with love by the team at
FIVE MILE
Alex, Niki, Rocco, James, Jacqui, Andy, Amy, Lyndal & Emily

Five Mile,
the publishing division of Regency Media
www.fivemile.com.au

First published 2019

Written by Jessica Sanders

Visit: www.re-shape.info

Illustrations by Stephanie Spartels


Author photo by Katja Kollecker



NATIONAL LIBRARY OF AUSTRALIA
A catalogue record for this book is available from the National Library of Australia

ISBN: 978-1-92597-003-6 (hbk)

Printed in China 5 4 3

# Dear Reader

I can't remember the first time I learned of the term 'self-care', but I do remember that I originally associated it with indulgence, bubble baths and a 'treat yo'self' attitude. It wasn't until three months into my first social-work role, when I found myself suffering from vicarious trauma, that I realised self-care wasn't an indulgence – it was essential. This experience forced me to make some tough decisions, ask for help, and prioritise my needs before anything else. All of this was self-care ... it just wasn't the kind I'd been sold.

When I wrote my first picture book, *Love Your Body*, I made sure to introduce children to the concept of self-care because I knew it was something that would support them their entire lives. Writing that book opened up lots of heart-warming conversations with people who, despite not being the book's target age group, resonated deeply with its messages of self-love and self-care.

Each of these people said they too needed to listen to their bodies, that they too needed to speak to themselves like their very best friend. It was through these conversations that *Me Time* was born. This is a book for you. Please don't hit rock-bottom before you start taking your own care seriously. Start right now. Give yourself permission to take your me time.

Your friend,

**Jess**

## AUTHOR'S NOTE

I would like to acknowledge that my perspective has been shaped by my social and cultural location as a white, middle-class, able-bodied, heterosexual woman. During the process of writing *Me Time* I have worked to balance my perspective by actively reading and listening to the different self-care practices of diverse individuals. I would also like to acknowledge the medical, political and academic roots of self-care. Lastly, I wish to acknowledge and thank some incredible thinkers, makers and doers who taught me about what it is to be human and why it is we need the care we do. Thank you to Bell Hooks, Brené Brown, Kristin Neff, Lillian Akenhan, Matt Haig, Oprah Winfrey, Roxane Gay, Sarah Blondin and Thomas Moore.

# How to use this book

It might sound strange, but it's true: sometimes we need a gentle reminder to take care of ourselves. And sometimes we need ideas to help us get started, to build our self-care routine and to encourage us along the way. That's where this book comes in.

This book is made up of four parts.

1. In the first section we'll explore the idea of self-care and define it as a holistic practice.
2. In the second section we'll explore the type of self-beliefs and ongoing work involved in setting up and maintaining a holistic self-care routine.
3. The third section is filled with self-care activities, which I have arranged by time. Time is always such a huge factor in our decision-making to commit to anything, let alone caring for ourselves. For this reason, I have organised self-care activities in timed sections: from one minute to half-day-plus ideas, you'll be able to find self-care that feels right for you and suits your schedule.
4. The final section is filled with resources designed to support your self-care, including checklists and recommendations for helpful online, book and app resources that I think you'll love.

When you see this symbol, it means the information on the page is research-based and that I have included information about the source material for further reading in the back of the book.

When you see this symbol, it means I've listed practical resources or a personal recommendation in the back of the book.

# CONTENTS

# What actually is self-care?

The term 'self-care' seems to be everywhere right now. It's widely used in advertising, where the term is often coupled with the idea of indulgence or pampering.

And while self-care can look like wearing a face mask in the tub, it's also so much more than that. Self-care can be crushing it at the gym one day and spending the whole day in your pyjamas the next. Self-care can be volunteering in your local community. Self-care can be setting healthy boundaries. Self-care can be simply getting enough sleep.

Ultimately, self-care is tuning in to your mind, body and spirit, and respecting what you find there. Self-care can be viewed differently, depending on your standpoint. For me, I see self-care as a practice, a holistic routine that incorporates all parts of the self. For this reason, I categorise self-care into four equal parts: care of the physical, mental, future and spiritual self. Envisaging self-care in this way treats it holistically, and also makes it easier to identify which part of yourself needs your focus. The four parts of the self are linked of course. When you care for one, the impact is felt by all at different levels.

The practice of self-care is contagious: one step in the right direction will lead to more. Committing to a self-care practice has the real potential to make you happier, healthier and more closely aligned with the life you want to lead. So, what are you waiting for? Keep reading!

# What I thought self-care was

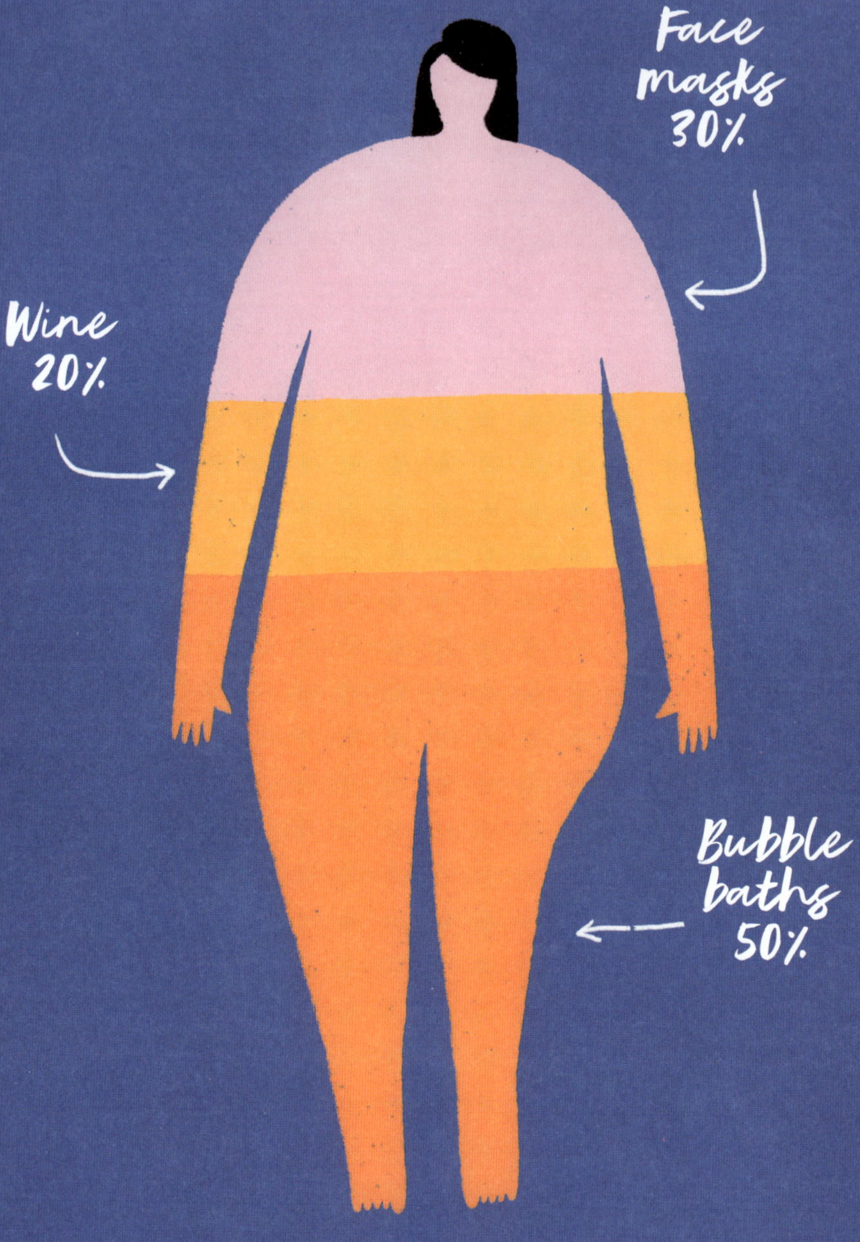

# What self-care actually is

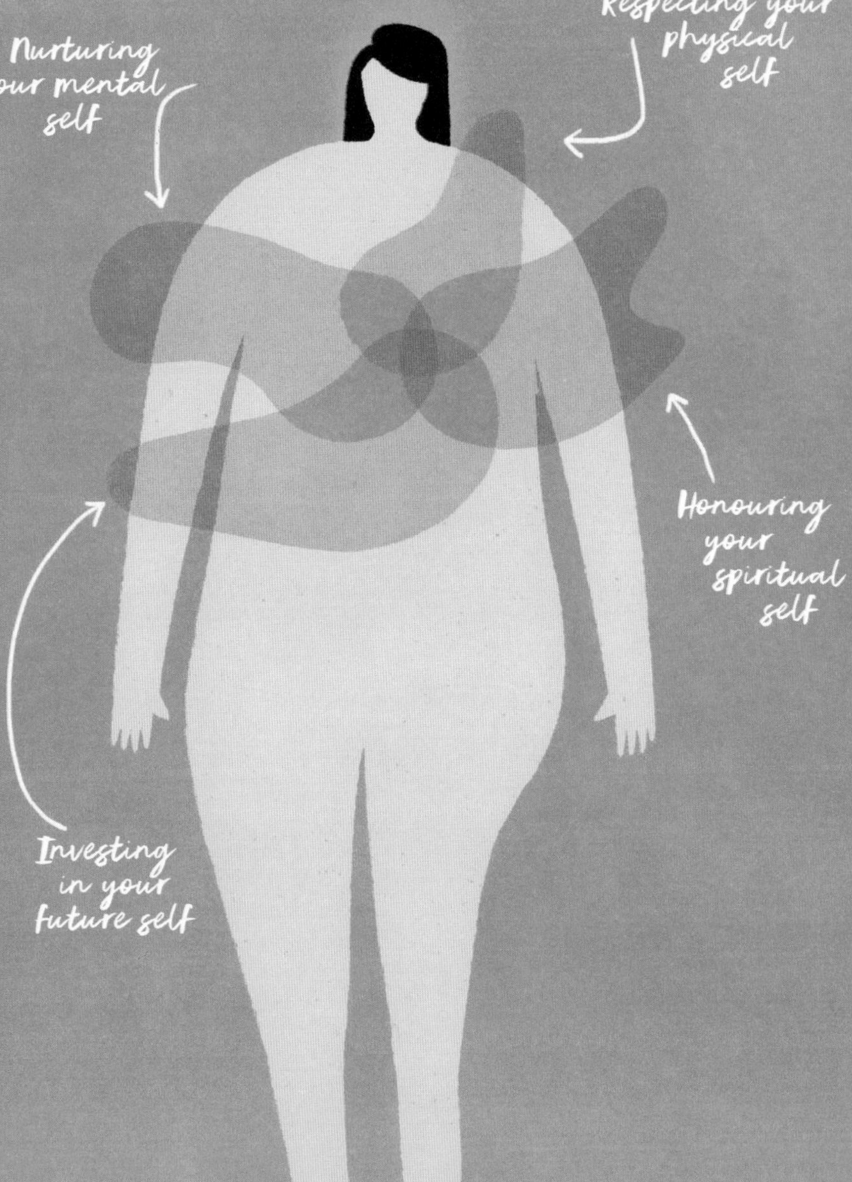

## Self-care is respecting your physical self

Hands up if, from time to time, you take your body for granted? Okay, I'm going to assume that you put your hand up because I most definitely did.

Time and time again we ignore the warning signals our bodies send us and push ourselves to the absolute limit. This is totally understandable. Our lives are crammed full of tasks, dramas and stressors, and it's all too easy to put the care of our bodies on the back burner. But all the excuses in the world don't make it okay. Consider this a little wake-up call – a reminder that we have got our priorities all wrong. Because our bodies are our most valuable resource. They enable us to experience all the beautiful things that life has to offer. Your body is your one true home. You don't get another, so it's essential to take care of it. When you fill your body with nutritious food, hydrate it and move it regularly, it will thank you! However, everyone and every body is different, and it's really important to find out what works for you. And let's face it: sometimes what your body really wants is a doughnut. So you should give it a doughnut! In other words, find what feels good for you and treat your body like the magical vehicle it is.

# Self-care is nurturing your mental self

Our brains are important. Those incredible cauliflower-looking things that live inside our heads control absolutely everything! But to the average person (i.e. not a neuroscientist) the brain's inner workings are a bit of a mystery.

When I experienced anxiety for the first time, it was a horrible feeling and I had no idea what it was. It wasn't until months later, when a friend introduced me to the term 'anxiety', that I was able to identify what was going on for me and seek help. The more I learned about my anxiety the easier it was to work through it and, at times, even prevent it. When we have a greater understanding of how our brains work we are better equipped to care for ourselves. The key to caring for the mental self is knowing when we need support from others, or from the experts. The mind is complex and asking for help is sometimes necessary to make sense of our experiences. Asking for help is an essential skill, and something most of us need to get a little better at.

Relationships are also a big part of keeping the mental self healthy, safe and happy. We are creatures of community and the single biggest determinant of our wellbeing is holding healthy relationships. Nurturing your relationships and building strong bonds is one of the best things you can do to take care of your mental self.

# Self-care is investing in your future self

Have you ever said, 'I'll deal with that later' or 'That's for future me to deal with?' I know I have! Turns out that 'future me' is still me – the only difference is that 'future me' has been sabotaged ... by me. Not cool, immediate me! When practising your self-care keep this scenario in mind. You must try to dance the line between being present and caring for your immediate needs and acting in ways that benefit your future self. For example, enjoy your morning coffee, but also try to reduce your daily caffeine intake because you're averaging four (double shots) a day, and that's too many for future self to stay healthy.

Self-care can also be caring for our glorious planet. Earth provides us with everything we need. So, it makes sense that when we care for the planet, we are also caring for ourselves, particularly our future selves. Remember that caring for the planet doesn't have to be all or nothing. No-one can do everything exactly right. Just start by doing something – little things, big things, whatever you can manage – to reduce your environmental impact.

Investing in your future self is the smartest decision you will ever make. Like any good investment, it requires your time and tapping into your wisdom to make informed decisions. After a little while you will begin to see returns on your investment. This might look like healthier relationships, a stable bank account or having more energy to do the things you love.

## Self-care is honouring your spiritual self

Spirituality means different things to different people. Many people connect to their spiritual self through religion, others do so by connecting with nature. There is no right answer, of course. Spirituality is deeply personal, and your spirituality can be as unique as you are. To nurture the spiritual self, it is important to create the time and space to connect with something bigger than yourself. This time is sacred, and it's just for you.

If you don't identify as spiritual, here are some helpful ways to identify this part of the self:

- that part of you that finds the beauty in nature
- that feeling of satisfied fullness after a night of dancing
- that warm glowing feeling that comes from spending time with people who love you
- knowing that you are just a small part of something bigger
- that inner drive to search for meaning
- that sense of joy that comes when you do what is meaningful to you

I think we can all recognise this part of ourselves that isn't just a brain and a body. It's something so much more wonderful than that. This part of ourselves is our spiritual self and it deserves as much love and care as all the other parts.

# I work at my self-care practice

The words 'work' and 'self-care' aren't ordinarily found together in a sentence. We typically think of work as what we are paid to do, and self-care as the thing we do outside work to make us feel better about working. I used to think about self-care in this way. It wasn't until I began my masters in social work that I truly understood self-care's essential and holistic nature. I learned that sometimes self-care can actually be hard work. Setting boundaries for yourself and your relationships, for example, can require discipline, commitment and ongoing work.

Some of the most important self-care practices are ongoing. This type of self-care can't be slotted into a time frame or pretty packaging, but it's often the most rewarding. These are the practices I explore in this section.

Each heading I've used in this section is an aspirational statement: self-beliefs we should be striving towards. It's important you know that most people are still working at this stuff, myself included. So try not to get caught up in perfecting self-care, just give it a go. I've included some handy prompts and examples so that you can begin integrating these practices into your daily routine.

# I know what I value and what I need

What do I value? What do I need? These are questions that we don't ask ourselves nearly enough. The answers to these questions are super important because they will directly inform your self-care practice. Figuring out what you value and need is your job, and yours alone. In a real way, this is the most important work you will ever do, because your answers directly impact all other areas of your life.

Sometimes we get caught in the currents of daily life, our obligations and other people's expectations of us. When this happens, it is easy to drift further and further away from what is important to us – what we value. Make sure to regularly ask yourself what you value. Asking this question of yourself when you feel adrift can bring you back to what is really most important and help to anchor you there.

What you need can change often. So it's a good idea to ask yourself what it is that you need regularly, and to keep your self-care routine flexible enough to accommodate this. Allowing flexibility in your self-care routine will help to give you what you need in the moment, rather than giving you what you assumed you might need. For example, you might have booked an exercise class, but you didn't sleep well last night and what you really need is a yummy dinner, your favourite TV series and an early night.

Give yourself permission to take what you actually need and let go of the fear that if you don't follow a strict schedule you are letting yourself down. That's simply not true. In fact, you'll just be more in touch with what you need and value and consequently where you want to go.

Keeping a journal will help you to clarify your answers to these questions.

Here are some prompts to get you started.

When I feel stressed I need to put everything in perspective.

When I feel tired I need to prioritise rest and give myself permission to do nothing.

When I feel anxious I need to find a quiet place and focus on my breath.

When I feel ..................... I need to .......................

When I feel ..................... I need to .......................

I value creativity so I will make a safe space for play.

I value connection so I will nurture my friendships.

I value empathy so I will actively listen to those around me.

I value..................... so I will ...........................

I value..................... so I will ...........................

# I prioritise my self-care

Once you've identified what you need and what you value, it's a lot easier to make time for those things. A busy life should not stop you from caring for yourself. Take these three steps to prioritise your self-care:

1. Schedule your self-care into your diary or phone calendar. Maybe use a different coloured pen or icon so it stands out. You are probably already doing some self-care activities as part of your daily routine without realising it – maybe even two hours' worth, which is ideal. But everyone's situation is different, so don't panic and avoid the temptation to throw this book across the room if two hours' self-care seems impossible!
2. To find more time for your self-care you may need to make some bold moves – cut out those unnecessary activities that are draining your energy and resources.
3. Have room to move. If you don't feel like doing the self-care activity you planned, then don't. Check in with yourself that day and pick a self-care practice that suits your needs in that moment. Of course, the better you know yourself, the better you can plan your self-care.

> **"When you recover or discover something that nourishes your soul and brings joy, care enough about yourself to make room for it in your life.**
>
> JEAN SHINODA BOLEN

## I say no

It feels so good. Yell it from the rooftops.

NOOOOOOOOOOOO!

No thanks.

Nope.

Nahhhh.

I'm good.

NO, I do not want to pick you up.

NO, I do not want to go out tonight.

NO, I do not want to get out of the bath.

And, while you are at it, stop apologising for things that don't require apologies!

There is freedom realising that you are the boss of you, that you have the autonomy and the right to say 'no' when you need to. This freedom provides you with the space and time to practise self-care.

Remember: saying yes can be fun too. Just make sure you find a happy medium between what you want to do and what you need to do. And remember, never feel guilty for saying no: your time is just as important as anyone else's.

> **When you say 'yes' to others, make sure you are not saying 'no' to yourself.**
>
> PAULO COEHLO

# I fill my own cup first

Your metaphorical cup is an indicator of your general wellbeing. When your cup is full, you feel content, satisfied and generally happy. When it's empty you feel drained, unfulfilled and can feel unwell. The self-care learning here is to keep your cup full by replenishing it every time that you pour from it. Filling your own cup first is not selfish, it's an essential part of being able to sustainably care for others. Think about your self-care like an aeroplane oxygen mask. You need to put on your mask first before you can help anyone else with theirs.

## ACTIVITIES THAT MIGHT DRAIN YOUR CUP:

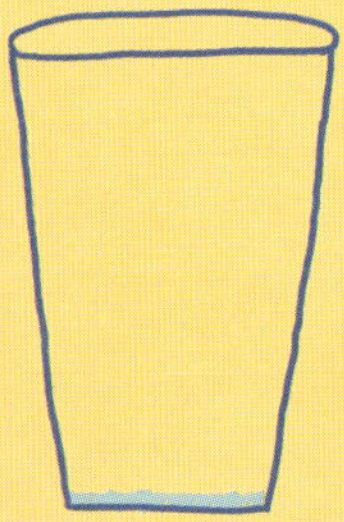

- Work related issues
- Break-ups
- Family issues
- Public speaking
- Health problems
- Lack of exercise
- Socialising
- Life in general

FILL YOUR CUP WITH THE GOOD THINGS IN LIFE.

# Balance is a myth.

**There is only the dance**
**we do in search of it,**

**the supplementing**
**and deducting,**

**the correcting and**
**re-directing,**

**this is where you will**
**find your bliss.**

# I accept myself

Most of us find it difficult to accept ourselves exactly as we are. There is always something we would change if given the chance. Self-acceptance means accepting yourself without conditions or exceptions. It requires acknowledging that we all have flaws and we have all made mistakes, and that none of those things define us. When we accept who we are, we are less likely to fall into the self-comparison trap. Comparing yourself to other people is a joy-thieving habit that a lot of us struggle with.

Self-acceptance is hard work. Not only do we need to battle our inner critic, we also have to navigate society's toxic message that we are not enough. That our lips aren't plump enough, our bodies aren't toned enough and our lives aren't aesthetically-pleasing enough. Accepting ourselves as we are is a powerful, and even political, act. When we know that we are enough we don't waste time, money and brain space chasing the things we've been told we should have.

**"In a society that profits from self-doubt, liking yourself is a rebellious act.**

CAROLINE CALDWELL

## BE YOUR OWN CHEERLEADER

Self-acceptance is tricky, and there will be days when you need to be your own cheerleader. Here are some things to tell yourself ...

### if you are struggling with self-acceptance:

- I'm an imperfect human just like everybody else
- Not every story I tell myself is true
- Mistakes help me to learn and grow
- I am enough just as I am

### if you are struggling to accept your physical self:

- I'm not here to be beautiful, I am so much more than that
- My body works hard for me every day
- My body is strong, my body is unique, my body is my own

Pick the one that resonates with you. Write it, cross-stitch it, paint it on a wall!

Accepting yourself doesn't mean you stop striving to grow, learn and evolve. Self-acceptance is the foundation from which self-esteem, self-love and other beautiful things can grow.

Finding self-acceptance might not be easy, but it's absolutely worth it.

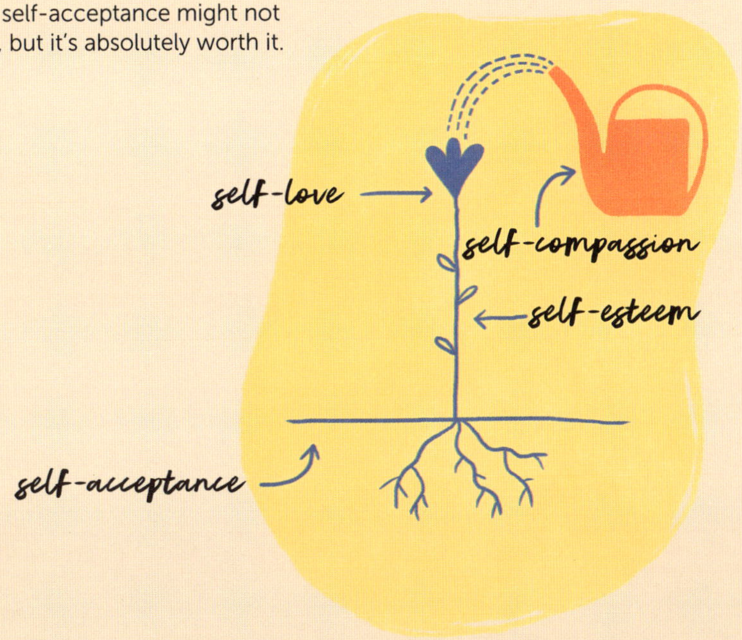

# I believe I am worthy of my own care

For some of us the biggest barrier to regularly practising self-care is the misguided belief that we do not deserve it. If you are feeling undeserving, remember that every single one of us is inherently worthy of love and care. No matter what. If you are finding it hard to believe these words today, try the exercise below to help you to reconnect with a desire to nurture yourself. If feelings of unworthiness are ongoing, please seek support from one of the organisations listed in the back of this book. Every single one of us deserves to feel that we are loved and worthy of care.

## ACTIVITY

Find a photograph of yourself as a child. If you don't have one close by, try conjuring an image of your younger self in your mind.

- What do you want for that child?
- Do you think that they are deserving of love?
- That child is you and you are still worthy of your own care.

If that activity feels too emotionally challenging, try some self-care that allows your body to feel safe and comforted, such as yoga. If we can't convince our mind that we are worthy, we can at least show our body. And remember, building our self-worth is an ongoing process so try to be patient with yourself.

> **You are worthy of the love you so willingly give to others.**
>
> UNKNOWN

# I speak kindly to myself

From childhood we are encouraged to be kind and compassionate to others, but rarely were we ever taught to extend that same kindness and compassion to ourselves.

Self-compassion is the act of speaking to yourself like you would your very best friend. It is how we should respond to our failures, to ourselves on those days when everything seems to be going wrong, and in the moments when we feel we are not enough.

A common fear among those of us reluctant to practise self-compassion is that without self-criticism we would never get anything done. However, positive reinforcement and compassion, not constant criticism, is what motivates us to work hard. That's just management 101.

**When you realise you are being your own worst critic, try these tactics instead.**

Ask yourself: 'Would I say this to a friend?' If the answer is no, think about what you might say to a friend in the same situation and apply this to yourself.

Ask yourself: 'Am I the first person to have done this or felt this way?' The answer to this question is, of course, no. Everything that we experience is a part of the collective human experience. When we remember that things will go wrong and that suffering is experienced by all, our inner critic grows quieter.

Engage in a self-care practice that comforts and soothes you. Even if you can't silence the inner critic immediately, you can show your body that you are safe and cared for through physical acts of self-compassion.

> **Let yourself be human. That's all.**
>
> CLEO WADE

# I cultivate self-awareness

Self-awareness is cultivated through the mental self but has incredible benefits for the whole self. Self-awareness is the ability to see yourself clearly, to know who you are and understand how others perceive you. Research tells us that those who are self-aware are more fulfilled, creative, confident and hold stronger relationships.

Practising self-awareness can, at times, feel uncomfortable, but it has the potential to relieve a lot of stress and anxiety for future you. When you are aware of how you work and who you are, it helps you to make decisions that best support and nurture you. Self-awareness is the key to building a life and community that's right for you, and what could be more self-caring than that?

## PRACTICES TO BUILD SELF-AWARENESS

- Meditation or mindfulness to quiet the mind
- Making a daily commitment to developing self-awareness
- Being both compassionate and honest with yourself
- Listening with an open mind to the constructive feedback of others
- Staying curious about how your mind and body work
- Avoiding thinking in black and white terms
- Identifying patterns in your thoughts and feelings

Researcher and psychologist Tara Eurich has studied self-awareness extensively, and in her research she discovered something surprising. Those who are self-aware don't ask 'why' when they self-reflect, they ask 'what'. She found that 'why' questions actually lead us further away from the truth and generally make us feel bad.

Here are some questions to promote self-awareness.

- *What is the most common emotion I experience each day?*
- *What is something kind that I do for myself?*
- *If my body could talk, what would it say?*
- *What is most important to me?*
- *What went well today and what didn't go well?*

If you are able to, write down your responses on paper. Journaling is a really effective way to cultivate self-awareness.

# I set boundaries

Setting boundaries might sound limiting. But it's not. It's actually the opposite. When we close the door on what harms us and limit what drains us, we open up a world of possibilities. Setting boundaries is an important part of self-care and, at times, it can be the most difficult practice. Boundaries should exist within the relationship you have with yourself as well as the relationships you have with others. Boundaries are a form of protection and prevention. We only have a certain amount of energy to give, and boundary-setting is a great way of protecting that energy.

Be sure to clearly communicate your boundaries with others. This will help you to establish expectations that reduce confusion and conflict. For example, you might be feeling a bit overwhelmed at work right now. What you really need this weekend is some time to decompress and recharge before Monday rolls around again. But your friends keep asking you to come out. Communicating to them how you are feeling and why it is you can't come out is setting a boundary. This clear communication will help your friends to realise it's not that you don't want to spend time with them, it's simply that you are preserving your energy and taking care of your mental health. And what friend wouldn't want that for you?

When we speak openly about our mental and physical health we are better able to understand and support one another. Starting a dialogue about your self-care practice will empower those around you to do the same.

## EXAMPLES OF BOUNDARIES

- Limiting time spent with people who drain your energy without giving energy back
- Not working outside of work hours
- Putting away technology when spending time with family and friends
- Standing up for yourself
- Surrendering to fatigue instead of fighting it

## A RECIPE FOR BOUNDARY-SETTING

### A full cup of self-awareness

Self-awareness is at the heart of boundary-setting as it allows us to set the boundaries that are right for us. Self-awareness also supports our ability to clearly communicate to others why it is we are setting boundaries.

### A sprinkle of self-discipline

We all need self-discipline in order to establish and maintain our boundaries. You'll slip up sometimes, and that's okay. Every time you make the decision to set or reinforce a boundary, you are strengthening your ability to do so next time.

### A heaped spoon of self-love

Self-love is your motivation to set and maintain boundaries. Love yourself enough to protect your energy and prioritise your needs. If you're not able to be self-loving at the moment, then try to set boundaries out of gratitude for all the things your body and mind do for you.

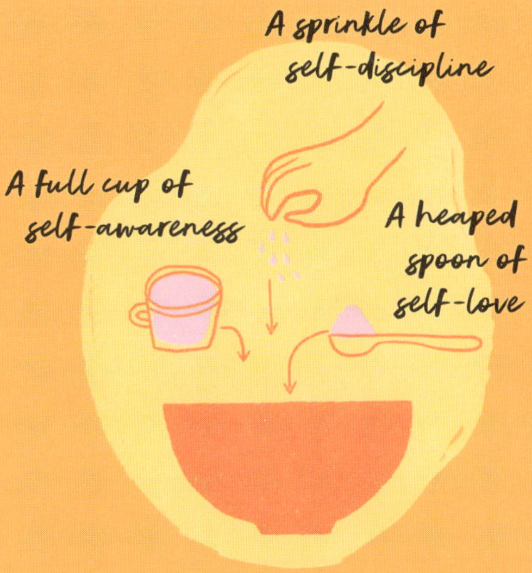


> **Boundaries are the distance at which I can love you and me simultaneously.**
>
> PRENTIS HEMPHILL

# I make time for my self-care

One of the biggest barriers to self-care is time. Sadly, there is no magic fix to find more than 24 hours in a day – and the old 'get up at 5 am' is just plain unhelpful for most of us. Realistically, to make time for your self-care, you will need to be both ruthless and creative. Ruthlessly cut out unnecessary activities that drain your time and energy. And be creative in finding time for self-care in and around the other aspects of life. If the idea of carving out time for self-care sounds easier said than done, answer this: can you find one spare minute?

From one-minute practices right through to half-day-plus activities, this section is filled with timed self-care. Use these ideas to build up, or build on, your self-care routine. Not every activity will resonate because everyone's self-care is different. And you may find that you have already been practising some of these activities without identifying them as self-care. This is important. When you reframe activities you're already doing as 'self-care practices', you completely change your relationship with them for the better. For example, that walk you take to the bus each morning becomes an opportunity to set intentions, listen to music or practise mindfulness.

> "One of the most valuable gifts you can give yourself is time."
>
> OPRAH WINFREY

# 1 MINUTE self-care

# Take a moment to thank your physical self

Too often we take our physical selves for granted. Our bodies carry us through our lives. They fight for us when we are sick and gift us the ability to experience life's everyday pleasures. Expressing gratitude towards our bodies is actually a great way of caring for the mental self.

A recent study found that expressing gratitude towards the body through writing leads to an improved body image.

Ask yourself: 'Which part of your body are you grateful for?'

Reflect on the answer to this question and then write your response down.

> ... and I said to my body, softly,
> 'I want to be your friend.'
> It took a long breath and replied,
> 'I have been waiting my whole life for this.'
>
> NAYYIRAH WAHEED

# Meditate

Unless you've been living under a rock, you've heard about meditation. This practice is common within several faiths, the most well-known being Buddhism. Today, meditation is practised outside faith communities all over the world. Meditation has the ability to reduce depression, boost the immune system, build concentration, and ease stress and anxiety.

Clearly, it's good stuff!

However, many of us don't feel we have the time or ability to quieten our minds. A one-minute meditation is the perfect introduction – by lowering the time commitment and your expectations, you remove the two biggest barriers to trying meditation.

Start a one-minute meditation by shutting your eyes and taking a brief moment to check in with how your body is feeling. Then slowly move your attention from the top of your head all the way down to the bottom of your feet. Bring an open and non-judgemental mind to this process. Notice how each part of your body feels as you scan over it. You could set a timer on your phone to mark the end of your practice.

To receive the full benefits of meditation, it should be a regular practice. I have included an app recommendation at the back of the book, which will support you to build a regular meditation practice.

# Release some tension

With so many of us now working primarily from our computers a tight neck is a common complaint. Relieve tension from your neck and care for your physical self with three easy stretches.

1. Start in a comfortable seated position. Place your left hand under your bottom so that you are sitting on it and place your right hand on the top left side of your head. Gently pull your head towards your right shoulder, hold the stretch for 20 seconds.
2. Now do the same thing but on the other side. Sit on your right hand and place your left hand on the top right-hand side of your head. Gently pull your head towards your left shoulder and hold for another 20 seconds.
3. For the last stretch interlock your fingers and cup the back of your head. Use your hands to gently guide your head forward, so that your chin moves towards your chest. Hold this stretch for a final 20 seconds.

# What three things made you happy today?

Research has found that writing about your happy moments can improve mood and significantly reduce visits to health-care services.

Take one minute at the end of the day to write down three joyful moments you experienced. It could be the steam coming off your coffee in the morning, or the cute dog you saw on your way to work, or the belly-laugh you had with a friend on the phone. Life can be full of beautiful moments if you just take a moment to be physically and mentally present for them.

# Do one task from your 'to-do' list

This one is for all the procrastinators out there. Have you ever felt so overwhelmed by everything you needed to do that you were unable to do anything at all? I know I have. Getting one small thing ticked off your to-do list can reduce the stress and anxiety felt by your mental self.

> **Self-care is how you take your power back.**
>
> LALAH DELIA

# Sign a petition

Self-care isn't always about me me me, it can also be about we! When we care for those around us it's not entirely selfless, because it also makes our mental self feel really good. Signing our name to a cause we care about is a great way to start caring for the wider community.

Spend a minute exploring the www.change.org website. There are always great campaigns running. Find an issue that is close to your heart and sign a petition to lend your support.

> **It is the greatest of all mistakes to do nothing because you can only do a little.**
>
> SYDNEY SMITH

# Drink some water

It might sound obvious, but so many of us forget to drink enough water throughout the day. Water is, of course, so important as it supports every function of the physical and mental self. GPs recommend about 6–8 glasses per day, but the amount of water you require will fluctuate depending on if you're in a hot climate or engaging in strenuous exercise. It only takes a few seconds to drink a mouthful of water. By my calculations, it will take you one minute to drink thirty mouthfuls. I'm not going to even try and do the math of how many litres that would be, but look, it's a good start.

These are my top tips for keeping hydrated:

- Get a reusable water bottle you like the look of. Let's face it, if it's a good-looking bottle you're much more likely to carry it around with you.
- Make sure your bottle has measures written on it, this is a handy way to keep track of your intake.
- Try to create the habit of regularly drinking throughout the day. I've recommended a free app in the back of this book that will send you regular reminders to drink water throughout the day if you think that would help you.

# Light a candle

Sometimes, transforming a standard daily activity into a nourishing self-care practice is just about changing the vibe! Lighting a candle signals that this moment, right now, is a little bit special. Candles also make your room or house smell delightful and give off a calming, warm light. They can also be integrated into your self-care rituals, for example, lighting a candle every time you have a bath or when you sit down to meditate.

# Perform a small act of kindness

When we do something kind for someone else, it helps us to get out of our own head and has a positive impact on our mental self. Plus, don't you want to live in a world where people are actively kind? I sure do.

You can never truly know what's going on in someone else's head. They might really appreciate your kindness today. Here are some quick and easy ways you can make the world a kinder place.

- Smile at a stranger
- Open a door for someone
- Let someone go before you in the shopping queue
- Pick up some rubbish on the ground and put it in the bin
- Cheerfully give way to a driver who is trying to turn onto the road
- Leave an uplifting note in a public place for someone to find
- Compliment someone on their energy and presence
- If you pass someone experiencing homelessness, make eye contact with them and give them what you can, even if it's just a kind word

**“We shall never know all the good that a simple smile can do.**

MOTHER TERESA

# Hug it out

Hugs are incredible for both your physical and mental self!

Hugs reduce stress and anxiety.
Hugs release a chemical called oxytocin (which makes us happier).
Hugs protect against illness.
Hugs improve heart health.

Ask someone if they would like a hug. If no-one is around, try giving yourself a hug and say to yourself, 'Hey, you're doing just fine.'

# 5 MINUTE
# self-care

# Use affirmations

An affirmation is a simple set of words designed to comfort and support your mental self. You can call on an affirmation whenever you need one. You could create your own personal affirmation, look for one online, or use one of these.

**My body is strong, and my body is my own.**

**I am grateful for all that I have.**

**Mistakes are how I learn.**

**I am enough.**

# Make space for daydreaming

When was the last time you actually just let yourself be bored? I'm personally terrible at this, the moment I find myself without anything to do I reach for my phone or laptop – every single time. This kind of behaviour is pretty terrible for the mental self because it doesn't allow our brains time to process all the information we take in each day. We are also robbing our mental self of the opportunity to daydream, and daydreaming actually serves an important function.

We typically associate daydreaming with laziness, but the activity that occurs in the brain when we daydream is actually highly rich and complex. Daydreaming can allow us to get into a 'flow state' of creativity where some of our best ideas are born. It's also a way of preventing dementia, so it serves both the future and physical self. If you'd like to learn more about why daydreaming is important I've included the link to a really interesting podcast episode in the back of the book.

Give yourself five minutes to do nothing at all and let yourself daydream.

# Flex your gratitude muscle

Gratitude is a buzzword for sure, but it is for good reason. A gratitude practice has the power to increase your happiness and overall life satisfaction, which is of course very beneficial to your mental self.

It's so easy to get caught up in what we don't have instead of focussing on all that we do have. Practising gratitude is not something we do intuitively. But the more we practise it, the more effortless it will become.

You could keep an ongoing list of all the things you are grateful for, create new lists regularly or write letters to yourself as a reminder of all that you have to be grateful for. Creating a gratitude ritual can also be powerful: run through all that you are grateful for while brushing your teeth or when you get into bed each night.

I am grateful for my home.

I am grateful that I have access to fresh fruit and vegetables.

I am grateful that I have access to education.

I am grateful that dogs exist.

# Tell an important person in your life why you are grateful for them

We often wait until a birthday or until someone is sick to tell them how much they mean to us. But why not tell them today? A couple of sentences sent via a text is all it takes. Kind and unprompted messages like these will make someone's day. Doing something nice for someone else helps you to get out of your own head and makes you both feel lovely – two things that your mental self will thank you for!

# Ask for help

If you're feeling down, overwhelmed or just confused reach out to someone you trust. Be mindful of the people you choose to be vulnerable with. Not everyone is worthy or capable of holding space for you. And remember, you can always reach out for professional help: just call one of the hotlines listed in the back of book and they will provide you with support and guidance.

# We all need to ask for help sometimes

# When life is too much, brushing your teeth is enough

We all have days when we don't have the motivation to do anything at all. Some of us have these days more than others – the weight of this feeling will vary depending on our mental health. When you are feeling like it's all a bit too much, try to perform small and simple acts of self-care like brushing your teeth, washing your hair or making yourself a cup of tea.

If your lack of motivation persists, the ultimate act of self-care is to seek support from a mental health-care professional. A great way to start is to call one of the hotlines listed in the back of the book; they will provide you with support and guidance.

# Organise your time

Feeling as though you are always running behind is not a nice feeling. Self-care is not always about caring for yourself in the present moment, it's also about caring for your future self. A few simple changes to your routine could remove a whole lot of stress for future you. For example, pack yourself lunch and some healthy snacks the night before work or allow an extra five minutes to get to an appointment so that you don't have to rush.

# Practise mindfulness

Ruth A. Baer describes mindfulness as the process of 'intentionally bringing one's attention to the internal and external experiences occurring in the present moment'. It is a form of meditation that can lead to amazing health benefits such as reduced anxiety, greater body satisfaction and an increased attention span. The great thing about mindfulness is that you can practise it anywhere, anytime.

Practise mindfulness while you are making your morning tea or coffee. Focus on the individual actions, smells and sensations of what you are doing – try to be present.

# Cuddle a pet

Cuddles from our furry friends are so beneficial for our mental and physical selves that there are actual services that provide pet therapy to people who are unwell. Studies have found that patting a pet can reduce your stress levels, improve blood pressure and calm your mind. If you're lucky enough to have a cute fluffer around go give them some love.

# Laugh

There is nothing better than laughing so hard that it hurts.

Laughter is literally medicine for our physical and mental selves. It has been shown to heal and prevent illness, alleviate pain, plus moderate stress and anxiety.

Take five minutes to have a chuckle with a friend or colleague. If you don't have someone around that makes you laugh, think of a movie, TV show or comedian that you find hilarious. Look up their funniest moments on YouTube and have a good giggle.

# Dance up a storm

A good dance session is a great way to quieten a busy mind. Not only is dancing a great form of exercise, it also positively impacts mood and energy levels and reduces stress.

Cue a couple of your favourite 'dancey' tracks and move your body just for fun! You might feel silly at first, dancing on your own, but after a little while you won't be able to stop the smile from creeping across your face. Remember, nobody is watching, and nobody cares, so just let your body move in whatever way it wants to without judgement.

> **Do something every day that is loving towards your body and gives you the opportunity to enjoy the sensations of your body.**
>
> GOLDA PORETSKY

# 10 MINUTE self-care

# Walk barefoot on the earth

I know walking on the ground with your shoes off in the name of health sounds like some made-up nonsense, but it's a legitimate thing. It's known as 'earthing' or 'grounding', and the benefits have been studied extensively. Physically connecting to the earth's surface is linked to better sleep and pain reduction. Apparently, this is thanks to the vast supply of electrons that exist on the earth's surface. I nearly failed science in school so I won't pretend to know what that means. I have however included some research in the back of the book if you'd like to find out more from some researchers that know their stuff.

Kick off your shoes and get outside. While you're doing this, try to be physically and mentally present with each step.

# Do some slow and mindful stretching

We usually associate stretching with something to do before and after a workout, but making stretching a regular part of your self-care routine will benefit your physical, mental and future self.

Focussing on how the individual parts of your body are feeling while stretching is a great way to practise mindfulness, and consequently reduce stress and anxiety. There are physical benefits to stretching as well, like increased flexibility and improved posture. Stretching can also help prevent your future self from injury.

Put on some comfy clothes, calming music, and even light a few candles if you're feeling fancy. Start with some simple stretches to get in touch with your body. If you're feeling tight in certain areas, spend a little more time in that particular stretch.

# Power nap

If you feel exhausted, stuck or unmotivated, try taking a quick power nap. Power naps are just like restarting a computer, they refresh the brain. A quick nap improves productivity, learning, memory, mood and creativity.

Find a quiet spot where you won't be disturbed for 10–15 minutes, which is the ideal time frame for power-napping. Set an alarm and give yourself permission to rest.

# Lie back and watch the clouds

Life can get so busy that sometimes we forget to stop and just look up. Cloud watching, or stargazing, can be a great way to calm our minds and gain perspective. Our worries can become small in comparison to the vastness of the sky and what lies beyond. Also, it's quite fun to find shapes and objects in the clouds and daydream.

Breathe

# Make time for self-reflection

There is a difference between self-reflection and self-deprecation. It's healthy to regularly engage in self-reflection: this is how we connect with ourselves, build healthy relationships and enhance our self-awareness. If your self-reflection becomes hurtful and overly critical, make sure you ask for support from someone you trust or from one of the hotlines listed in the back of this book.

To distinguish between self-reflection and self-deprecation, ask yourself: are you reflecting because you want to learn and grow or are you doing so because you think you're not good enough?

At least once a month sit down with a cup of tea, and spend 10 minutes reflecting on the following questions:

**Am I leading with kindness and empathy?**

**If my body could talk, what would it say to me?**

**Am I making time for the things I value most?**

# Experiment with aromatherapy

Aromatherapy is the use of essential oils to bring about physiological and emotional changes. Oil burners or diffusers are common ways of using essential oils. A few drops into water is all that is needed. Here are a few common ways essential oils can be used to care for the physical and mental self.

**Lavender: good for sleep, very calming**

**Sandalwood: supports mental clarity**

**Chamomile: calms the nerves and alleviates anxiety**

**Peppermint: helps to boost energy levels**

**Rose: soothing for grief and loss**

# Tune in to what your body needs

Our bodies are constantly sending us messages. The more we listen to them, the clearer those messages will become. You may find that your body needs a vegie-packed meal or that it is craving rest.

For 10 minutes sit or stand in a quiet place and listen to your body. Bring a curious and non-judgmental mindset as you ask yourself how your body is feeling right now. Then, if you can, give your body whatever it needs.

"You aren't doing 'nothing' when you choose to put your wellbeing first. In fact, this is the key to having everything.

BRITTANY BURGUNDER

# Balance your news intake

On any given day there will be more good things happening in the world than bad things. But that can be easy to forget when watching the news or scrolling through Facebook. Negative news gets the most clicks. In a world where we are consuming more content than ever before, it's far too easy to start going down a negative news rabbit hole.

Be proactive about seeking out positive news in order to balance out the content you are consuming. One way of doing this is to visit the goodnewsnetwork.org online to read heart-warming and hopeful stories from all over the globe. If you enjoy what you find there, sign up to their newsletter to receive the top good news stories each morning. Another way is by filling your social media feeds with pages and accounts that prioritise good news (aka cute dogs). I've included a few of my favourites in the back of the book.

I think we all need a regular reminder of the good that exists in the world. Even if it's not 'newsworthy', lots of good and kind things do happen each day, keep an eye out for them.

# Save the planet one cup at a time

Did you know that one standard takeaway coffee cup is lined with plastic, and takes more than fifty years to decompose in landfill?

Taking care of our planet is also taking care of your future self. Remember that you don't have to be vegan or living a one-hundred per cent plastic-free lifestyle to do something about climate change. Do what you can, and don't let the misguided idea that you have to be perfect at saving the planet stop you from taking action.

Save the planet in 10 minutes or fewer by switching your takeaway paper cup to a reusable one. Buy a cool reusable cup online or dig around in the back of your cupboard for an old mug and keep it in your bag for when you need it. Some cafes offer a discount to reusable-cup users – so you can save money and the planet.

# 30 MINUTE

# self-care

# Work through a problem on paper

Writing is a really effective way to nurture the mental self. The process of writing helps you to clarify your thoughts, feelings and increase self-knowledge. Writing is also great for the physical self. Writing about negative experiences and trauma has been found to strengthen the immune system and reduce health problems.

Writing about an issue you may be facing can provide you with a new perspective and help you to develop valuable problem-solving skills. There doesn't have to be structure in your writing. Just write down whatever is running through your mind. Write for as long or as little as you like. You will know when you're finished because a weight will be lifted off your chest.

# Give yourself time to be sad

Nobody can be happy all the time and it's normal to experience the inevitable ups and downs of life. Despite this, I think a lot of us feel pressured to be happy all the time or 'put on a brave face'. And this makes sense at work or at school, but repressing emotions just does not work in the long term. The kindest thing you can do for your mental self is provide the time and space to feel the full spectrum of your emotions.

Don't rush yourself. If you're feeling sad, give yourself at least 30 minutes in a safe and comforting space to feel those challenging emotions.

If you find that these emotions are stopping you from living your life in the way you would like, then the best thing to do is seek support. Reach out to someone you trust or contact one of the hotlines listed in the back of this book.

Everything is

going to be okay.

# Write a letter to your future self

Writing a letter to your future self will help you to make decisions that positively impact future you. It's also a great way to reconnect with your goals and aspirations, which will help keep you on track to achieving them.

Spend half-an-hour writing to your future self, covering the following topics:

- What do you hope for your future self?
- What would you like to see happen in the future?
- What do you want to be different to how it is for you now?

When you have finished your letter, stick it in an envelope and address it to your future self. You could even specify an age when you would like to read it. Put the letter away somewhere safe and forget about it for now.

# Create a new ritual

In the context of self-care, a ritual is an action or set of actions that cares for any one of the four parts of the self. A ritual can be performed daily or repeated at longer time intervals. Having your own rituals can be very comforting and an effective way to acknowledge a time, place or event.

You might already have your own rituals. For example:

- a religious practice and/or celebration
- a skin-care routine
- visiting your favourite coffee shop before work
- cleaning on the first day of spring

If you don't have your own rituals, why not create some? It could be as simple as reading the paper on Sunday mornings or meditating each night before bed. Designing our own personal rituals can help to make the everyday sacred.

# Take a break from reality

We hear a lot about the negative aspects of video games, but there's a positive side to them too. Playing a game for a healthy amount of time is a great way to unwind and give your mental self a break from reality. Gaming with others is also a great way to meet people and connect online.

# Do it, pamper yourself

## MAKE A HOME-MADE FACE MASK

Home-made face masks are an affordable way to treat your skin to a 'spa day' from the comfort of your own home. Also, sometimes it's less about the face mask and more about the act of spending time and energy on yourself.

### Mix your mask

1/2 ripe avocado
1 tsp. plain yogurt (use coconut yogurt for a vegan option)
1 tsp. honey (use agave for a vegan option)

Mix all the ingredients together and apply to your face. Leave the mask on for 10–15 minutes and then use warm water to remove it.

## PAINT YOUR NAILS

Shaping and painting your nails can be a soothing activity as it requires focus and repetitive movements. Plus, everything is made better when your nails are looking glorious. Put on a podcast or some tunes and enjoy the process. If you're terrible at painting your nails (I absolutely am) and if you are able to afford it, take yourself to your local nail salon and support a small business.

# Eat a big-ass bowl of pasta

Pasta has to be one of the most comforting meals to ever exist. Do you know why it tastes so damn good? Because it is full of carbs, and carbs are an integral part of the human diet. Gluten-free friends – I see you, I feel you. Luckily, there are some tasty gf options out there now, so nothing can hold you back from slurping on some spaghetti.

# Move your body

Exercise is an investment in your future self. Exercising for 30 minutes a day, five days a week will literally increase your chances of living longer. We were made to move and, when we do, our physical and mental selves thank us by protecting us from illness and making us feel happier by producing endorphins. If you are feeling down, try to get up and move your body. Even just a gentle walk will help you feel better.

Be sure to find a form of exercise you enjoy – there is no point pursuing exercise you don't like because you won't keep doing it. Swimming, running, boxing or bike-riding are all great ways to move your body.

And yoga is gentle on the body and good for long-term exercise into your nineties! It's okay if you can't commit to an everyday practice. Instead try working exercise into your daily routines. For example, bike-riding to work instead of driving, walking to work instead of catching public transport or taking the stairs instead of the escalator.

> **Find what feels good.**
>
> ADRIENE MISHLER

# 1 HOUR self-care

# Watch an episode of *Queer Eye*

This is probably one of my favourite self-care activities and one that I could not resist including in this book. I love *Queer Eye* because it is the ultimate feel-good reality TV show, and because encouraging others to practise self-care is a big part of the show. Equip yourself with some tissues, tasty snacks and settle in for the wonderful ride that is *Queer Eye*. The Fab Five will have you laughing one second and crying the next. I promise that you are going to walk away from this show with your heart warmed and your faith in humanity restored.

# Take a long bath

Baths can be super relaxing, but different people relax in different ways. Do your bath your way. You might want to read (or listen to) a book as you soak in the tub. Or maybe light some candles and play music. It doesn't matter what you do as long as you max relax!

# Go to therapy

Your mental health is a priority and it's just as important as your physical health. If you have the ability, take yourself to see a counsellor, psychologist or therapist. A session will typically run for one hour, and it's common to have appointments once or twice a fortnight.

Often times, people think they have to be really unwell before seeking help, but that's just not true. The best time to see a mental health-care professional is as a preventative measure. You can always stop going if you feel you don't need their counsel anymore. But it's comforting to know that there is someone out there for you when you need them. Don't waste months or even years asking yourself, should I go? Invest in yourself and your future today.

If you're not quite sure about the process of finding a mental health-care professional that's right for you, speak to your GP or contact one of the hotlines listed in the back of the book. They will be able to walk you through the process and provide you with helpful resources.

# Take a long, leisurely walk

Walking is not only great for your physical health, it's also excellent for your mental health. As you're walking, take note of your surrounds and try to focus on the beauty in what you see. An hour-long walk is also the perfect opportunity to reflect and process what's going on in your head.

# Clean

For some people, cleaning can be incredibly therapeutic. A clean and organised space can help to create a clear and calm mind. It can also provide us with a sense of accomplishment which, in turn, motivates us to do other stuff. Put on some music or a podcast and get to cleaning. (If you are in need of podcast recommendations I've included my favourites in the back of the book.)

# Read a book

Books transport us to faraway places and can act as a refuge from the ups and downs of day-to-day life. They can help us to understand another's perspective, increasing empathy and tolerance. Reading has incredible health benefits too – it reduces stress, improves sleep and even helps to prevent Alzheimer's disease.

Ask a librarian or bookseller for recommendations to find books that excite and intrigue you.

## Time spent reading is time well invested.

# Learn more about your brain and body

When you have a greater understanding of how your brain and body work it becomes a lot easier to understand yourself and others. At the back of the book you will find the links to some books and clips that will get you started. I suggest keeping a notepad by your side and taking notes. Educate your friends or family on what you've learned. It will help you solidify this information in your own mind as well as sharing the knowledge with your favourite people.

# Feed yourself like you would feed someone you love

There's so much information out there about what we should and shouldn't be putting into our mouths. It's hard to know what to believe and it's easy to get swept up in the latest fad diet or 'cleanse'. As someone who once tried every diet under the sun, my advice is this – don't diet, don't overthink eating.

Food can be fuel, medicine, pleasurable or a combination of all three. Food is not 'good' or 'bad' and nor are you 'good' or 'bad' for eating certain foods. Essential vitamins and minerals exist in our food and we need these to live happy and healthy lives.

Food does not just feed the body, it feeds the brain as well. There is a direct link between our gut and our brain. If our gut is unhappy, our brain will be affected and vice versa.

When you are preparing food for yourself, try to have fun with it. Ideally you should include three different coloured vegies, some grains, and meat or a protein-packed alternative. However, if you are feeling like something not particularly nutritious – then listen to your body and eat it guilt free. Above all else, try to feed yourself out of a desire to respect, love and care for your body.

# Put on an outfit that makes you feel like a boss

Sometimes putting on the right outfit can give you that extra confidence boost you need to get out the door and take on the world. Dress to reflect how you are feeling or how you  would like to feel. Putting time into how we present ourselves is not selfish, it's self-care.

# Marie Kondo your Instagram

If you've never heard of Marie Kondo, she's a cleaning guru with several bestselling books and a Netflix show all on the topic of 'tidying up'. Her method is simple, she asks you to pick up an item in your home and ask yourself if it brings you joy? If the answer is yes, you keep it. If the answer is no, thank that item for all it's done for you and say goodbye. I strongly suggest you go through a similar process with the accounts you follow on Instagram.

Go into your 'following' list and as you scroll down ask yourself – does this account bring me joy or does it make me feel bad about myself?

If the answer is 'makes me feel bad about myself' then thank that account or influencer for whatever it is they have done for you, and then click 'unfollow'.

Cleansing your account of negative influences can have a transformative effect on your mental self. Why not try following some positive accounts to make your feed feel like a safe and uplifting space?

I've listed some of my favourite positive accounts in the resources section at the back of the book.

# 2 HOUR
# self-care

2 HOUR SELF-CARE

# Manage your money

If you've ever struggled with money you know that it can take a huge toll on your mental, physical and future self. The way we manage our money will directly impact the quality of our life. Many of us are not taught how to manage our money, which is madness considering the important role it plays in our lives. If you're someone who struggles to save or is unsure about your financial situation this activity is a great starting point for you.

You'll need a pen, four different coloured highlighters, a blank piece of paper, and a printout of your bank statement dating back one month.

LET'S GET STARTED

## FIGURE OUT YOUR FINANCIAL SITUATION.

Draw four columns and write one of these headings per column: Earn, Spend Essentials, Spend Personal, Save. Use your statement and four pens to turn your transactions into a dollar-value per column:

- Your 'Earn' column is the total amount you earn each month.
- Your 'Spend Essentials' is the total amount you spend on essential items like rent, groceries, bills, loan repayments etc.
- Your 'Spend Personal' amount is the non-essential items like coffees, meals out, accessories etc.
- And your 'Save' is, you guessed it, the amount you put into long-term savings.

## SET YOUR GOALS

What is it that you're saving for? Do you want to save a deposit for your first home, do you want to travel around Europe, do you want to adopt a doggo? Write down your goals, then next to them write down how much it will cost to achieve that goal.

## CREATE YOUR BUDGET & START SAVING

Now that you have the important calculations, you'll be able to create a budget or saving plan that will allow you to work towards your goals. There are some great budgeting books and apps out there. I've recommended a few of my favourites in the back of the book.

# Take a break from technology

We are more connected than we ever have been before, and there are so many different ways that we can reach one another. Technology has created a culture where we feel obliged to respond quickly and stay up-to-date with what everyone else is doing. Sometimes that can all get a bit much and it's important to give yourself breaks from being 'on' all the time. Your phone has a 'do not disturb' function – don't be afraid to use it. You are the boss of your time and you don't owe anyone a response.

# Let there be light!

Everyone deserves to have their own space that feels safe and comforting. Lighting is a huge part of setting the mood in a space. When creating a warm and safe space for yourself, consider giving your room a 'lighting' makeover. You won't regret it. Salt lamps, regular lamps, mood lamps, fairy lights and candles – whatever kind of lighting you choose just make sure it gives off a warm light.

# Discover new places

Jump on a bus, train, in a car or on a bike and venture to some place new. You don't need to go far to find somewhere you've never been before. Discovering new places close to home can evoke a sense of adventure and improve our sense of connectedness to our community. If you are lucky enough to be able to travel to faraway places, this is also an incredible way to learn, grow and unwind. Travel can also gift us valuable perspectives and insights into ourselves and others.

Here are some fun adventure ideas:

If you like history and architecture go to a historic town. Walk around and admire the buildings, read those tiny plaques that tell you their history. Don't forget to eat some tasty treats and read a book in a cafe.

If you like the beach, head to the ocean and watch the waves roll in. Bring a journal with you and write about whatever comes to mind. Why not top off your day with fish and chips?

Plan a solo trip overseas. When I was 19, I spent two months travelling Southeast Asia on my own. I was terrified at first, but it was one of the best things I ever did. If you're privileged enough to be able to save for a trip overseas then get yourself on a plane asap!

2 HOUR
SELF-CARE

# Start a compost bin

Caring for the planet is inherently caring for ourselves and our future. A simple and effective way to take care of our planet is to start a compost bin. The waste we produce each day goes into landfill, which then creates carbon emissions ($CO_2$). These $CO_2$ emissions trap solar energy in the atmosphere, contributing to climate change. A compost bin turns waste, which would normally go into landfill, into amazing soil. If you don't have your own vegie patch, you can donate the soil you create to your local community garden. Returning composted soil to the land increases carbon in the ground, reducing the effects of climate change.

LET'S GET STARTED

5 easy steps to becoming a composting household:

1. Do a quick Google to find a composting system that works for your home. Take note of the processes involved by writing them down or printing them off.
2. Go to the local hardware to purchase said system plus a little bin to collect your food scraps in the kitchen.
3. When you get home set up your new composting system outside. Definitely do not set it up inside – they can smell like a schoolbag with a three-week-old banana at the bottom of it. Put your little bin in its new home under the sink or on the bench.
4. Print off a list of things that can and cannot be composted and stick it to your fridge. You'll find some cute lists available for free download on Pinterest, just search 'what to compost'.
5. Tell the other members of your household how your composting system works so that everyone knows what to do. You could also add the instructions to the fridge until it becomes second nature.

Congratulations! You are now a composting household and a friend of the earth! Future you just did a little happy dance in celebration.

# Create a vegie patch

Gardening is beneficial for your physical and mental health and has been found to reduce symptoms of depression and anxiety. This makes it a great self-care activity. Plus, there's nothing more satisfying than eating fruit or vegetables that you've grown yourself. Not only do they taste so much better, but it's also great for the planet and your bank account.

Spend a couple of hours creating your own vegetable patch. If you don't have a garden, what about using lots of little pots or repurpose some apple crates? Maybe you could even join a local community garden. There are so many different ways to create a vegie patch and heaps of DIY blogs online to help you get started.

# Celebrate the little wins

It's important to take the time to acknowledge and celebrate your achievements, no matter how small you may think they are. The monumental achievements aren't the only ones worth recognising. Life happens in between the big wins, and it's important to celebrate the journey, not just the destination. The more we celebrate the little wins, the more we realise how much there is to be grateful for. Being grateful nurtures the mental self.

**"Your work will never be finished.
Your inbox will never be empty.
Your body will never be perfect.
Your striving will never end.
Don't race life. Walk it.**

MATT HAIG

# Catch up over coffee

When we get really busy our social life is sometimes the first thing to go. Quality time spent with a friend is a great way to care for the mental self and something we should always prioritise. Invite a friend out for coffee and give yourselves at least two hours for a proper catch up. If your friends are supportive they will work around your schedule or understand your mental/physical health status and adapt plans accordingly.

# Find a creative outlet

Fear of failure is often the thing that stops us from creating. The thing about creative expression is that you cannot fail at it. Creativity exists in the act of exploration and making. It's so beneficial to your mental self, as being creative releases dopamine, which makes you happy. Creativity is also an investment in your future self by increasing brain function and reducing the chance of dementia.

Try to remove any expectation of productivity before you start creating, and if you're trying out a new medium give yourself at least two hours to play around and experiment. Remember, you don't have to show anyone your creations – create for yourself and have fun with it.

And don't give me that 'I'm not creative' nonsense. As a human being you are inherently creative. Humans have been creating since prehistoric times.

### Some ideas to get you started

- Start a knitting or crochet project
- Create a mixed media collage
- Paint or draw that which inspires you
- Write poetry, stories or letters to express and work through your feelings
- Use a camera to see your world a little differently
- Get creative in the kitchen by trying a new recipe
- Create a dance routine to your favourite song
- Play a musical instrument, sing or do both

# Take yourself on a self-care picnic

Pack a bag filled with your favourite snacks, a book or journal, a picnic blanket and head outside. If you can, turn your phone off, so that you can be really present. This is your time – it does not need to be shared with anyone else. The most important relationship you will ever have is the one you have with yourself, so it's super important that you learn to love your own company. If you're someone who struggles to be comfortable in solitude, then I strongly recommend you get yourself a copy of *What a Time to be Alone* by Chidera Eggerue to read on your self-care picnic.

> **Time spent with yourself is never time wasted.**
>
> CHIDERA EGGERUE

# HALF-DAY + self-care

# Volunteer!

Volunteering is a great way to get out of your own head and help others in need. Research has found that volunteering can have a positive impact on depression and improve overall life satisfaction and wellbeing.

Constant exposure to the news and all the terrible things it highlights can get pretty overwhelming. The reality is, we can't solve all the world's problems – each one of us can only do what we can do. When volunteering, it's probably best to find one issue you are passionate about, something where your contribution can make a difference. And remember, you don't need to have a whole day available – even a half-a-day a fortnight can make a big difference! There are all kinds of individuals and organisations that need your specific set of skills. Have a look online to find the perfect volunteer opportunity for you or go out and make your own.

**As you grow older, you will discover that you have two hands, one for helping yourself, the other for helping others.**

MAYA ANGELOU

# Get lost in a good book

Remember that holiday you loved? The one where you basically just slept, ate and read for a whole week? We shouldn't have to wait until we're on holiday to spend all day reading. Make time to flop into a comfy chair and get lost in a good book. Your mental self will love you for it.

# Put on a spread

A dinner party is a great way to bring you and your friends together. They are also a way of caring for the mental self because they combine creativity and connection. I love a good dinner party – my friends have recently started calling my kitchen 'The Jesstaurant', that should tell you how much I love it. It gives me a lot of joy to be able to cook for the people I love. It's how I show them just how grateful I am for their friendship.

LET'S GET STARTED

Jess's checklist for the ultimate dinner party:

- First things first, decide on your dish. Pick something that is filling and scalable. My personal favourite dish is okonomiyaki – a Japanese pancake. It's cheap to make, filling and a crowd favourite. I've included a link to an easy recipe in the back of this book. ☼
- Do the grocery shopping first – no-one needs the stress of a last-minute dash to the shops.
- Clean up – you have guests coming! This is also just a good excuse to freshen up your home.
- Set the table – oh no, you don't have enough plates?! Ask your bestie to bring some over.
- Lighting is everything ... a few candles and lanterns go a long way in setting the mood.
- Pre-cook as much food as you can. Once everyone arrives, you'll get distracted and probably burn something.
- Wine, you'll be needing wine. Ask your friends to bring a bottle or four. Under the drinking age? Swap this out for something delicious or non-alcoholic.
- Put your phones away, talk about small and big ideas, enjoy each other's company, be present.

# Go for a hike

The simple act of being in nature relieves mental fatigue, strengthens the right hemisphere of the brain and restores harmony to the functioning of the brain as a whole. Contact with nature has been found to positively impact blood pressure, cholesterol, outlook on life and stress-reduction.

Hiking is a great way to connect with nature and move your body. You could grab some friends or go it alone. If you do decide to hike solo make sure you're prepared and let someone know where you are going. If you've never gone on a hike before, there are some great hiking blogs and websites listed in the back of this book to get you started.

While you are hiking try to focus on all that you are seeing and hearing. Think about the seeds that had to grow and the time that had to pass in order to create this natural environment. If you really start to think deeply about nature and how it came to be, it's hard not to experience a feeling of genuine wonderment – a state of awed admiration and respect.

# Design your own 'you day'

Design a day filled with your favourite activities. For me a 'Jess Day' involves going to the local Lebanese bakery for coffee and a spinach pastry, followed by an op-shopping extravaganza. I finish up with a long walk through a leafy park. What's yours?

A 'you day' is a way to recalibrate and to reconnect with what you enjoy, which is a big part of what makes you who you are. You shouldn't need to think too hard about these days, just fill them with your favourite things! Call on these days whenever you are feeling a little disconnected from what makes you, you.

# Transform into a creature of comfort

Sometimes (a lot of the time for me) you just need a lazy night-in. Here are a few steps to achieving the ultimate lazy night-in taken straight out of the Jessica Sanders lazy-night repertoire:

**Have a shower or leisurely bath and get into some clean, comfy clothes.**

**Apply a face mask or do some kind of pampering activity.**

**Order takeaway or cook some simple comfort food.**

**Pour a glass of your favourite beverage (wine for me, please).**

**Turn on some 'trashy' TV or settle in for a movie marathon.**

**Soak it all up and let yourself enjoy this time – guilt and FOMO free. You deserve it.**

# I support my self-care

On one day, your self-care might appear as challenging self-work. The next day, it could look like spending the entire day in your PJs. Your self-care practice does not need to be perfect and nor do you. Don't over complicate it – don't make self-care another chore or an obsession. If you act from a place of respect and love for yourself, then you are doing self-care exactly right. That being said, sometimes it's nice to get a little reassurance that you're on the right track. For this I've included daily, weekly, monthly and yearly checklists. I've also included a bunch of further reading recommendations that will support your self-care and expand your knowledge of certain self-care concepts.

## Self-care reflective checklists

PHOTOCOPY THESE LISTS AND TICK AWAY.

# A DAY

Did you ...

- ○ **do something just for you?**
- ○ **say a kind word to yourself?**
- ○ **eat three meals plus snacks, and drink some water?**
- ○ **have one meaningful conversation?**
- ○ **move your body?**
- ○ **thank your body for all it does for you?**
- ○ **give yourself permission to be with your feelings?**
- ○ **stop and notice your surroundings?**
- ○ **find beauty in a single moment?**
- ○ **forgive yourself if you didn't do everything on this list?**

# A WEEK

Did you ...

- ○ **spend quality time with people you love?**
- ○ **hug someone?**
- ○ **learn something new?**
- ○ **have some alone time to reflect?**
- ○ **do something nice for someone else?**
- ○ **go into nature?**
- ○ **express yourself creatively?**
- ○ **make time to do nothing?**
- ○ **sleep enough?**
- ○ **forgive yourself if you didn't do everything on this list?**

# A MONTH

Did you ...

- ○ work towards a goal, and forgive yourself if you didn't quite make it?
- ○ perform small acts of kindness?
- ○ care for the environment?
- ○ connect with your wider community?
- ○ keep an open mind?
- ○ practise empathy?
- ○ experience immense joy?
- ○ say 'no' when you didn't want to do something?
- ○ spend some time writing to work through an event or emotion?
- ○ do something just for fun?
- ○ forgive yourself if you didn't do everything on this list?

# A YEAR

Did you ...

- ○ push yourself out of your comfort zone?
- ○ reflect on what you need and what you value?
- ○ articulate what you want and work towards it?
- ○ back yourself?
- ○ articulate and then reinstate your boundaries?
- ○ respect your body by listening and acting?
- ○ put your health first?
- ○ feel fulfilled?
- ○ forgive yourself for mistakes?
- ○ learn and grow from your mistakes?
- ○ forgive yourself if you didn't do everything on this list?

## Research-based further reading

**Some information in this book came from the research of others.**

**p. 13** *Harvard Study of Adult Development* is one of the longest-running studies on happiness and is still ongoing. Read more at https://www.adultdevelopmentstudy.org/

**p.31** K.D. Neff & K.A. Dahm's 2015 article 'Self-compassion: What it is, what it does, and how it relates to mindfulness.' Read more at https://self-compassion.org/wp-content/uploads/publications/Mindfulness_and_SC_chapter_in_press.pdf

**p.32** T. Eurich's 2017 TED Talk: Increase your self-awareness with one simple fix Watch it here: https://www.ted.com/talks/tasha_eurich_increase_your_self_awareness_with_one_simple_fix?language=en

**p.33** T. Eurich's 2017 book *Insight: Why we're not as self-aware as we think, and how seeing ourselves clearly helps us succeed at work and in life.* Find it at the library or your favourite bookstore.

**p.40** J. Dunaev et al.'s 2018 article 'An attitude of gratitude: The effects of body-focused gratitude on weight bias internalization and body image' published in *Body Image*, Vol 25, 9–13. Available online via: https://www.sciencedirect.com/science/article/abs/pii/S1740144517302991

**p.41** R.J. Davidson et al.'s 2003 article 'Alterations in brain and immune function produced by mindfulness meditation' published in *Psychosomatic Medicine*, Vol 65, 564–570. Available online via: https://www.ncbi.nlm.nih.gov/pubmed/12883106

**p.42** C. O'Keefe Osborn's 2018 web article (medically reviewed by T.J. Legg, PhD, CRNP), 'Ways to ease neck tension'. Read more at: https://www.healthline.com/health/neck-tension#treatments

**p.43** C.M. Burton & L.A. King's 2004 article 'The health benefits of writing about intensely positive experiences' published in *Journal of Research in Personality*, Vol 38, 150–163. Available online via: https://www.sciencedirect.com/science/article/nbspii/S0092656603000588

**p.49** E. Cirino's 2018 web article (medically reviewed by K. Cross, FNP, MSN) *What are the benefits of hugging?* Read more at: https://www.healthline.com/health/hugging-benefits#1

**p.54** S.M. Toepfer et al.'s 2012 article 'Letters of gratitude: Further evidence for author benefits' published in *Journal of Happiness Studies*, Vol 13, 187–201. Available online via: https://doi.org/10.1007/s10902-011-9257-7

**p.60** R.A. Baer's 2003 article 'Mindfulness training as a clinical intervention: A conceptual and empirical review' published in *Clinical Psychology: Science and Practice*, Vol 10, 125–143 Available online via http://www.wisebrain.org/papers/MindfulnessPsyTx.pdf

**p.60** J. Cho's 2016 web article '6 scientifically proven benefits of mindfulness and meditation'. Read more at: https://www.forbes.com/sites/jeenacho/2016/07/14/10-scientifically-proven-benefits-of-mindfulness-and-meditation/#20e8e9d863ce

**p.61** M. Carter's 2015 article in *Independent* 'Why having a pet is good for your health'. Read more at: https://www.independent.co.uk/life-style/health-and-families/features/how-having-a-pet-can-make-us-healthier-a6792126.html

**p.62** W.B. Strean's 2009 article 'Laughter prescription' published in *Canadian Family Physician*, Vol 55, 965–967. Read more at: https://www.cfp.ca/content/55/10/965.short

**p.63** M. Zajenkowski et al.'s 2015 article 'Let's dance – feel better! Mood changes following dancing in different situations' published in *European Journal of Sport Science*, Vol 15, 640–646. Available online via: https://www.researchgate.net/publication/265683087

**p.66** G. Chevalier et al.'s 2012 article 'Earthing: Health implications of reconnecting the human body to the Earth's surface electrons' published in *Journal of Environmental and Public Health*. Read more at http://dx.doi.org/10.1155/2012/291541

**p.67** S. Lindberg's 2018 article (medically reviewed by D. Bubnis, MS, NASM-CPT, NASE Level II-CSS) 'Stretching: 9 benefits, plus safety tips and how to start'. Read more at https://www.healthline.com/health/benefits-of-stretching#benefits

**p.68** P. Maquet et al.'s 2002 article 'Be caught napping: you're doing more than resting your eyes' published in *Nature Neuroscience* Vol 5, Issue 7, 618–619. Read more at https://www.cin.ucsf.edu/~houde/coleman/mednickNV.pdf

**p. 68** C.E. Milner & K.A. Cote's 2009 article 'Benefits of napping in healthy adults: impact of nap length, time of day, age, and experience with napping' published in *Journal of Sleep Research*, Vol 18, 272–281. Available online via: https://onlinelibrary.wiley.com/doi/full/10.1111/j.1365-2869.2008.00718.x

**p.74** B. Ali et al.'s 2015 article 'Essential oils used in aromatherapy: A systemic review' published in *Asian Pacific Journal of Tropical Biomedicine*, Vol 5, 601–611. Available online via: http://www.sciencedirect.com/science/article/pii/S2221169115001033

**p.80** K.A. Baikie & K. Wilhelm's 2005 article 'Emotional and physical health benefits of expressive writing,' published in *Advances in Psychiatric Treatment*, Vol 11, 338–346. Available online via https://www.cambridge.org/core/journals/advances-in-psychiatric-treatment/article/emotional-and-physical-health-benefits-of-expressive-writing/ED2976A61F5DE56B46F07A1CE9EA9F9F

**p.89** A. Semeco's (MS, RD) 2017 web article 'The top 10 benefits of regular exercise'. Read more at https://www.healthline.com/nutrition/10-benefits-of-exercise#section1

**p.96** S. McMains & S. Kastner's 2011 article 'Interactions of top-down and bottom-up mechanisms in human visual cortex' published in *Journal of Neuroscience*, 12;31(2):587–597 Available online via: https://www.ncbi.nlm.nih.gov/pubmed/21228167

**p.97** Healthline's 2016 article 'Five ways reading can improve health and well-being'. Read more at https://www.huffpost.com/entry/five-ways-reading-can-imp_b_12456962

**p.99** M. Clapp et al.'s 2017 article 'Gut microbiota's effect on mental health: The gut-brain axis' published in *Journal of Clinical Practice*, 7: 987. Read more at https://www.health.harvard.edu/diseases-and-conditions/the-gut-brain-connection

**p.108** NASA website. Read more at https://climate.nasa.gov/causes/

**p.109** S. Wakefield et al.'s 2007 article 'Growing urban health: Community gardening in South-East Toronto' published in *Health Promotion International*, Vol 22, 92–110. Read more at https://academic.oup.com/heapro/article/22/2/92/558785

**p.112** A. Stahl's 2018 web article 'Here's how creativity actually improves your health'. Read more at https://www.forbes.com/sites/ashleystahl/2018/07/25/heres-how-creativity-actually-improves-your-health/#35d31a5513a6

**p.112** J.N. Wilford's 2014 article 'Cave paintings in Indonesia may be among the oldest known'. Read more at https://www.nytimes.com/2014/10/09/science/ancient-indonesian-find-may-rival-oldest-known-cave-art.html

**p.116** C.E Jenkinson et al.'s 2013 article 'Is volunteering a public health intervention? A systematic review and meta-analysis of the health and survival of volunteers' published in *Public Health*, 13:773. Available online via https://www.ncbi.nlm.nih.gov/m/pubmed/23968220/

**p.119** C. Maller et al.'s 2006 article 'Healthy nature healthy people: "contact with nature" as an upstream health promotion intervention for populations' published in *Health Promotion International*, Vol 21, 45–54. Available online via: at https://academic.oup.com/heapro/article/21/1/45/646436

**I wish to thank and recognise the authors of the wise words quoted throughout this book.**

## Resources and Recommendations

**Sharing is caring. Here are great resources to support your self-care.**

**p.41** Smiling Mind have a free meditation & mindfulness app. Find out more: https://www.smilingmind.com.au/

**p.46** Drink Water Reminder N Tracker app Find out more: https://apps.apple.com/au/app/drink-water-reminder-n-tracker/id870372885

**p.53** All in the Mind podcast ep, called 'Dementia, sleep and daydreaming'. Listen here: https://podcasts.apple.com/au/podcast/all-in-the-mind-abc-rn/id73330911

**p.76** My fave good-news sources:

- **@the_happy_broadcast** illustrates the world's good news stories
- **@bodiposipanda** is the most colourful and positive activist on Instagram
- **@tunameltsmyheart** is the cutest doggo with the most biggest overbite
- **@wolfgang2242** is a beautiful soul who adopts & cares for elderly dogs

**p.96** My top podcast recommendations:

- **Shameless** – a pop culture podcast for smart women who love dumb stuff, hosted by Australian journos Zara McDonald and Michelle Andrews.
- **TED Talks Daily** – big ideas condensed into short daily episodes.
- **All in the Mind** – an ABC podcast that looks into the mind, brain and behaviour.
- **The Daily** – a *New York Times* podcast that delivers the biggest news stories in 20 minutes, 5 days a week.

**p.98** TED Talks has curated a helpful range of video playlists all on the brain. Watch here: https://www.ted.com/topics/brain

Here's some great books to read:
*How the Mind Works* by Steven Pinker
*The Brain that Changes Itself* by Norman Doidge

**p.101** Jess's Fave Instagram Accounts: @l_weigh @rachel.cargle @chessiekingg @cleowade @mattzhaig

**p.104** For some great finance information:

- App: **Raiz** – invest your spare change from everyday purchases into a diversified portfolio.
- App: **Pocketbook** – a budgeting app that allows you to identify exactly where your money is going.
- Book: *The Barefoot Investor* by Scott Pape is easy to follow and will empower you to save for your dreams.
- Podcast: **She's on the Money** – money expert Victoria Devine shares her foolproof tips for financial freedom.

**p. 116 Find a volunteer opportunity:**
https://govolunteer.com.au/
https://www.volunteeringnz.org.nz/

**p.118** Here's my fave okonomiyaki recipe: https://www.japancentre.com/en/recipes/1-okonomiyaki-savoury-pancake

**p.119** https://www.trailhiking.com.au/ A go-to website for hiking and gear advice, plus you can explore locations for your next hike! https://lotsafreshair.com/ A blog full of bush-walking and hiking tips from an 'unexpected outdoors chick'.

## Support hotlines

**In Australia**

Kids Helpline: 1800 55 1800 (Support for under-25s)

Beyond Blue: 1300 22 4636 (Mental health support and advice)

Lifeline: 13 11 14

**In New Zealand**

Youthline: 0800 37 6633 (Over the phone support for under-25s)

Lifeline: 0800 54 3354

Suicide Crisis Helpline: 0508 82 8865